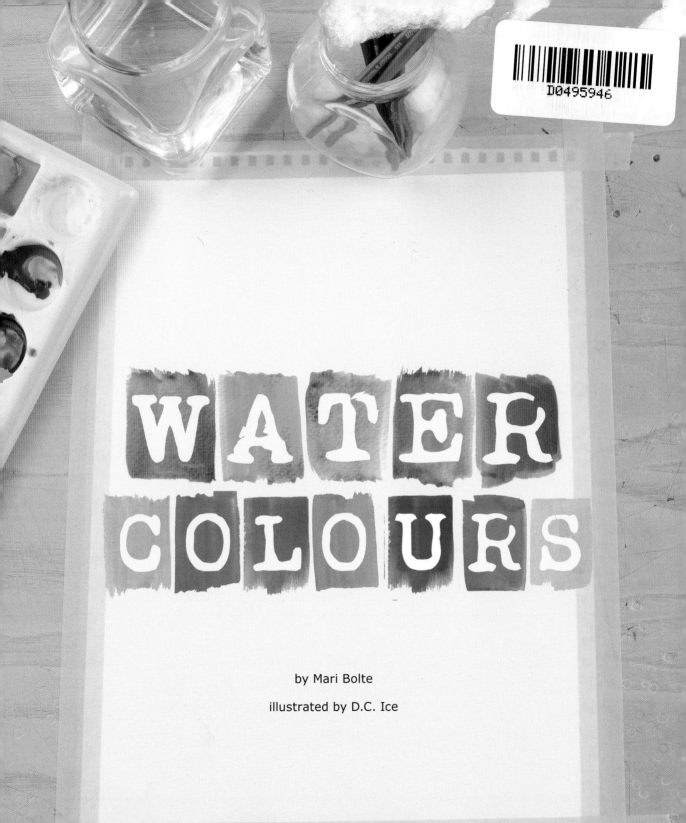

WATER COLOURS

by Mari Bolte

illustrated by D.C. Ice

Raintree is an imprint of Capstone Global Library Limited, a company incorporated in England and Wales having its registered office at 7 Pilgrim Street, London, EC4V 6LB – Registered company number: 6695582

To contact Raintree please phone 0845 6044371, fax + 44 (0)1865 312263, or email myorders@raintreepublishers.co.uk. Customers from outside the UK please telephone +44 1865 312262.

Text © Capstone Global Library Limited 2015
First published in paperback in 2014

UK editor: James Benefield
Designer: Bobbie Nuytten
Production: Laura Manthe
Printed in China by Nordica
0614/CA21400912
ISBN 978 1 4062 7981 8
18 17 16 15 14
10 9 8 7 6 5 4 3 2 1

British Library Cataloguing in Publication Data
A full catalogue record for this book is available from the British Library.

Photo Credits:
Illustrations by D.C. Ice; All photos by Capstone Studio and D.C. Ice except the following: Shutterstock: 501room, 6 (bottom), 9 (bottom right), donatas1205, design element, ffolas, 5 (bottom), Ivancovlad, 6 (top), Kess, 9 (top), Robert_s, 6 (top left), Roxana Gonzalez, 4 (top left), songquan Deng, 30 (bottom), Stephen Rees, 10 (bottom left)

We would like to thank Robert A. Williams, Instructor of Commercial and Technical Art, South Central College, North Mankato, Minnesota, USA, for his valuable assistance.

All the internet addresses (URLs) given in this book were valid at the time of going to press. However, due to the dynamic nature of the internet, some addresses may have changed, or sites may have changed or ceased to exist since publication. While the author and publisher regret any inconvenience this may cause readers, no responsibility for any such changes can be accepted by either the author or the publisher.

Contents

IN YOUR ART BOX

Along with crayons and markers, watercolours are some of the first art mediums young artists choose. Watercolours are easy and inviting to use. They can convey the artist's feelings with the flick of a brush. Express your thoughts with just a drop or two of water.

Paints and pigments

All paints are made up of a pigment and a binder. Pigments are dry, coloured powders. They can be natural or artificial. They can come from plants, animals, the earth or a lab. Pigment is what colours all painting mediums. The only difference between paint mediums is the binder that is used.

Binders are adhesive liquids that hold pigment. Pigment reacts differently depending on the binder that is used. This is why one colour of oil paint looks different than the same colour of watercolour paint.

WATERCOLOUR PAINTS

From the earliest times, artists painted with watercolours. Primitive artists mixed natural pigments with water or binders like animal fat to decorate personal items or draw the things around them. Today artists use vivid blends of colour to paint the world in watercolour.

Watercolours are made with pigments mixed with a binder called gum Arabic. Gum Arabic can be thinned with water. Because of this, watercolours dry quickly and are easy to clean up.

Watercolours are sold in pans or in tubes. Pan watercolours are sold as dry cakes. Tubes hold thick, paste-like paint. Both pan and tube watercolours need to be thinned with water before use. The projects in this book were created with both pan and tube watercolours.

The best kinds of watercolour paints are professional grades. Student grade watercolours are more affordable. However, the quality and consistency are not as reliable.

Some pigments, such as cadmium and cobalt, are toxic. Be careful when working with these pigments. Keep paint away from the mouth and eyes, avoid skin contact whenever possible, and make sure your work space is well ventilated.

5

PAPERS

Watercolour paper is the most common painting surface. This special paper is designed to absorb water evenly and slowly. It comes in different textures, from smooth, fine-textured paper to bumpy handmade pieces. It should be made of 100 percent cotton or linen. Fine- or medium-textured paper is best for beginners.

Watercolour paper also comes in a variety of weights, from 150 to 638 grams per square metre (72 pounds to 300 pounds). Thinner paper is less expensive, but also more likely to wrinkle. Many artists stretch their watercolour paper if they are using thinner weights, to prevent wrinkling.

Other commonly used surfaces for watercolours include rice paper, pre-stretched panels, parchment paper and thin fabrics.

COLOUR PALETTE

Watercolour paints come in many premixed colours. However, most artists start with a base palette of between eight and 12 main colours. Below is a list containing some of the more common colours:

French Ultra Blue, Permanent Purple, Cadmium Yellow, Veridiun, Winsor Blue, Winsor Green, Yellow Ochre, Paynes Gray, Brown Madder Alizarin, French Ultramarine, Cadmium Red, Lamp Black, Burnt Sienna, Prussian Blue, Raw Sienna, Indian Red, Alizarin Crimson

Do not store brushes upright. Water can seep into the bristles, causing them to spread. Water will also damage the handles.

BRUSHES

There are many brushes you can use for watercolour painting. They come in a variety of shapes and materials. Natural fibres are the best. The very best brushes are made of 100 percent Russian kolinsky sable hair. Buy the best brushes you can afford, even if you're just starting out. Natural brushes can be expensive. However, a set of quality brushes can last for many years if cared for properly.

Brushes should be cleaned after every painting session. Always handle brushes gently, and always lay them flat.

Different bristles serve different purposes. Flat brushes can make wide strokes or fine edges. Round-tip brushes can be used for almost everything, from bold washes to light detail. Wide or narrow brushes can paint thick or thin lines. Try a variety of brushes to find out which you like best.

Some powerful pigments may stain your brushes. This is OK – just make sure to get all the binder off your brush.

Washing brushes

Rinse brushes well in lukewarm water. Use a mild soap to lather the brush. Then swirl the bristles on your palm. Rinse and repeat lathering until no colour remains. Wipe gently with a clean rag and let the brushes dry. Store your brushes in a covered drawer or box to keep them clean. Keep brushes with mothballs to prevent moths and other insects from eating your brush bristles.

Round   Flat   Liner   Fan

Dot flower bouquet

Get friendly with watercolour! Test the waters by
practising wet-onto-wet and wet-onto-dry techniques.
Then create a bouquet pretty enough to give to
someone special!

2

4

5

1 Lay paper flat and tape down. Brush paper with water until it no longer absorbs water.

2 Use a round tip brush to apply thinned paint onto paper. Create dots of varied shapes and sizes.

3 While paint is wet, outline the flowers with darker shades. Add flower petals using the same technique. Colours should bleed into each other. Layer details to your liking.

4 Add stems. Allow the paint to dry.

5 Apply wet watercolours over dried flowers. Experiment with shading and texture. Allow the paint to dry.

6 Use a black felt-tip pen to draw leaf details and outline flowers, if desired.

The amount of water you add will affect how much your paint bleeds. Try working with various amounts of paint or water.

Always have at least two containers of water available. One container of clean water should be used for mixing paint. The other should be used to rinse brushes.

9

Mixed media

Watercolour paint is fun to experiment with. It reacts differently to many objects. It's easy to move around the page. It shows up on many surfaces, including coloured paper and wood. It is easy to thin and can be blotted or smeared. It dries quickly. Once dry, it can be painted over, rubbed or scratched off. It also works well with other mediums. Search your art box for simple supplies and experiment layering them with watercolours.

Painting techniques:

~**Wash** A wash is a thin layer of paint spread over a large area. Washes are painted in layers. This creates depth and detail.

~**Glazing** Apply a wash. Allow wash to dry completely. Add another layer. Continue as many times as desired.

~**Graded wash** Follow instructions for applying a wash. Instead of reloading your brush with paint before every stroke, reload with water. The finished wash will be dark at one end and light at the other.

Glazing

Applying a wash

Choose a colour. Mix the paint, taking care to blend it evenly. Be sure to mix enough for your project.

Begin at the top of the space you want to paint. Tilt the paper slightly. This will encourage the paint to run towards the bottom of the page.

Apply the wash with a wide stroke, working left to right. The colour should run to the bottom of the stroke, creating a bead of liquid. Recharge the brush, and apply the next stroke. Be sure that the top of the new stroke touches the bottom of the old stroke. The bead should run to the bottom of your new stroke. Continue applying the wash, working the bead down the painted area.

flat wash   *graded wash*

~**Wet-onto-wet** Use layers of wet paint to experiment with colour mixing and colour intensity.

~**Dry brush** Use a moist paintbrush but do not thin the paint with water.

~**Scumbling** Lightly paint one colour over another, using a fairly dry brush. The underlayer should still be visible.

~**Detail painting** Use a thin liner brush to add details such as outlines or edges.

~**Push out pigment** Lay a wet, used brush over wet paper. Allow the wet paper to pull the colour out of the paintbrush.

~**Watercolour pencils** Use water-colour pencils over wet or dry paint.

Wet on Wet

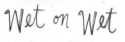

Dry Brush

Watercolour pencils

Push out Pigment

Scumbling

Detail Painting

glue

crayon

Paint over:

~**Glue** Create a pattern with PVA glue. Allow the glue to dry. Then paint over the dried glue. Your pattern will show through the paint. This is called resist painting.

~**White or coloured crayon** Use crayon in place of glue for another kind of resist painting.

~**Wood** Use unfinished wood instead of paper.

~**Black or coloured paper** Use black or coloured paper instead of regular watercolour paper.

~**Negative painting** Paint over waterproof objects such as leaves, tape or stencils. Once paint is dry, lift or remove the object.

Wood

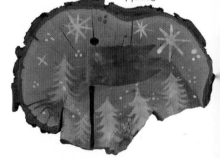

Black Paper

Negative Painting

11

Wet thread

Dry thread

Salt

fabric

Place on wet paint:

~**Wet thread** Lay wet pieces of string or thread onto wet paint. Remove once paint is dry.

~**Dry thread** Lay dry pieces of string or thread onto wet paint. Remove once paint is dry.

~**Salt or sand** Sprinkle onto wet paint. Blow or brush off once paint is dry.

~**Fabric** Lay or press pieces of fabric onto wet paint. Remove once paint is dry.

~**Wet paint** Drop paint onto wet paper or wet paint.

~**Hessian** Press hessian onto wet paint. The hessian will soak up paint and water, leaving a pattern behind.

Drop colour on Wet colour

Mix paint by swirling the brush through the paint. Mixing with the tip of your paintbrush is hard on the brush's bristles.

Hessian

Bubble Wrap

Lace

Paint onto:

~**Hessian** Paint hessian with watery paint. Press hessian onto paper to leave a design.

~**Stamps** Paint stamps and press onto paper.

~**Bubble wrap** Paint bubble wrap and press onto paper.

~**Lace** Soak lace in watercolours and press firmly onto paper. Use more than one piece to create layers.

~**Sponge** Dab sponge in watercolours. Then dab onto paper.

~**Bread** Soak up paint with bread. Then blot or dab onto paper.

Dab or rub wet paint with:

~**Fabric** Dab or wet paint with pieces of fabric. A rag or an old T-shirt will soak up extra liquid. The pigment will be left behind.

~**Feathers** Use a feather in place of a paintbrush.

Rub dry paint with:

~**Rubber** Rub dry paint with rubber.

~**Sandpaper** Lightly scratch away pigment with sandpaper.

Experimental cupcakes

Take mixed media a step further and create art good enough to eat! Texture brings depth and detail to your paintings. Test it out and create cupcakes that amaze!

Bubble Wrap

Sponge

Leaves, Grass or Herbs

Hessian

Bubble Wrap

Sandpaper

Watercolour Pencils

Strange things you can find at home

Peacock Feather

Stretching watercolour paper

Lighter-weight watercolour paper needs to be stretched before you start this project. Otherwise, the paper may warp while it dries.

Dip paper into a pan or bucket of water. Make sure it's wetted evenly. Remove the paper. Use a sponge to absorb excess water.

Place the paper onto your work surface. Pin or tape it down with craft paper tape. Use a sponge to smooth the paper and remove any wrinkles or bubbles. Once the paper is completely dry, it is ready to paint.

For most of these cupcakes, start by laying down a wash. Press your material of choice onto the paint. The material can be removed once the paint has dried.

For other cupcakes, try painting directly onto the material. Then blot or press the material onto already-dried watercolour. Test out different amounts of paint. Try using more than one colour at a time.

Brush feathers through wet paint or rub sandpaper over dry. See which technique you prefer.

Painting over an object can create a reverse effect.

This is another great project to experiment with the wet-onto-wet and wet-onto-dry techniques.

Add even more detail to your cupcakes with fine paintbrushes or watercolour pencils. Try re-wetting the paper afterwards to soften the new lines.

Straw draw

Think out of the box by applying watercolour without brushes! Start with a simple graded wash. Then use a straw to drip and blow paint across the page. You'll have a spooky forest in no time!

1 Wet the paper thoroughly.

2 Using a fan brush, sweep the paint across the bottom of the paper.

3 Wet the paintbrush before applying each new stroke. Each stroke should be lighter than the last. Continue until the entire paper is covered. Allow to dry completely.

4 In a cup, mix water and a small amount of black paint. It should look like darkly coloured water.

5 Dip a straw into the cup. Use the straw to drip coloured water onto the bottom of the paper.

6 Blow through the straw to push the coloured water around the paper. Each drip will create a tree branch.

7 Dip a paintbrush into the coloured water. Use it to create a base for your spooky trees.

Stylish Mr Fox

There are many ways to paint the same object. Pick one object and challenge yourself to paint it in three styles – realistic, stylized and abstract. Can you do it?

Realistic

1 Outline the fox's eyes with a black liner brush.

2 Use a wash to paint the fox's orange fur.

3 Paint the fox's black legs.

4 Thin the black paint to create a lighter grey tone. Use this grey to paint the fox's chest and facial features.

5 Use a liner brush to add depth to the fox's fur. Add various shades of orange with small strokes. The more strokes you add, the thicker the fur will become.

If your paint looks dull, you're probably not using enough water.

What's the difference?

Realistic: The Realist movement lasted from around 1850 to 1870. Realist paintings try to show the expressiveness of real life. Look up works by Honoré Daumier and Gustave Courbet.

Stylized: Stylized art falls somewhere between realistic and abstract. Stylized art shows what the artist sees through his or her eyes. See Art Nouveau (1800–1914) and Post-Impressionism (1880–1915.)

Abstract: Abstract art began in the early 1900s. Artists used simple shapes and colour palettes. They wanted to paint in a freer, more creative way. See Cubism (1907–1920s), and works by Salvador Dali and Jackson Pollock.

Stylized

1 Outline the fox's eyes with a black liner brush. Add three black strokes for the legs.

2 Load the liner brush with orange paint. Use it to outline the fox.

3 Use a round tip brush loaded with darker orange paint. Add colour under the fox's eyes and to its snout.

4 Thin the black paint to a light grey. Add the fox's fourth leg. The lighter paint shows that the fox's leg is in the background.

5 Continue adding details with the liner brush.

6 Add spots in shades of orange with a small round tip brush.

Abstract

1 Use a liner brush to paint one large eye and one small eye.

2 Connect the eyes with a line. Paint another line at an angle. This will be the fox's nose.

3 Paint a sweeping line between the fox's eyes. Add an ear at each end of the line. Finish outlining the fox's face.

4 Add a tail.

5 Paint the fox's legs.

6 Add more fur to the fox's face and tail with a liner brush.

7 Add spots with a small round tip brush.

Chinese brush painting

Brush painting originated in China. It quickly became popular throughout South East Asia. Brush painters use a special ink made of soot and glue. When thinned with water, the ink is called sumi. Brush paintings are traditionally made on rice paper.

Chinese brush painting, also known as *sumi-e*, is a simple and beautiful way to paint with watercolours. Each stroke is "final" – once painted, it cannot be corrected.

1 Thin brown and blue paint in your watercolour tin. Dip your brush into both paints, and paint the tree branch. Paint as much as you can at once.

2 Use quick, short brush strokes to paint the outline of the bird.

3 Use longer and thicker strokes of orange to paint the bird's belly.

Chinese brushes have bamboo handles. The brush is made of absorbent, natural hairs. Each brush is thick and pointed. The harder the brush is pressed, the thicker the painted line will be.

4 Add orange flowers to the branches with light paint strokes. Use darker shades of orange to add depth and shading.

5 Paint the bird's beak. Add light washes of orange to give your bird more life.

21

Shapely stars

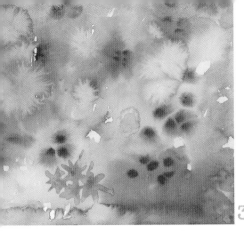

3

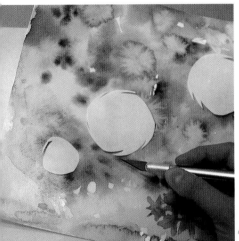

4

5

7

Explore the world of positive and negative shapes. Washes, wet-onto-wet techniques and contact paper will help you create a multilayered piece of art. Use this project to play with colours, shapes, patterns and brush strokes.

1 Thoroughly wet paper with water.

2 Use a fan brush to sweep green paint over the entire paper.

3 Drop wet purple, yellow and blue paint randomly onto the paper. Allow the paint droplets to spread naturally. Let it dry.

4 Use a craft knife to cut circles out of contact paper. Cut stars out of the circles. Set stars and circles onto the now-dry paper.

5 Place the stars and circles however you like. Then remove backing and stick the shapes onto the paper.

6 Sweep dark blue paint over the entire page. Let it dry.

7 Peel contact paper off watercolour paper. Discard.

8 Use white paint to decorate the collage.

Use the heaviest paper possible for this project; 300 gsm (140 pound) or thicker is best.

Limited palette

Some artists say to paint what you know. Others teach to paint what you see. Why not do both? Get up close and personal with an object that you probably know well – your mobile phone.

Limit yourself to a palette of just a few colours. Then get to work personalizing your phone!

Applying thinned transparent paint over a dry wash is called glazing. Using multiple glazes makes rounded objects look great. Use the side of your brush to add shadows to your mobile phone's screen.

1 Draw two rectangles with rounded corners.

2 Saturate your brush with water. Use pink to paint the hibiscus flowers onto the case and the phone screen.

3 Blend peach paint into the pink to give the flowers more depth. Let it dry.

4 Paint thin, black lines inside the flowers. Add speaker and button details to the mobile phone.

5 Dot the flowers with pink and peach paint.

6 Paint the mobile phone screen blue. Using a contrasting colour will help the flower stand out.

Undersea wash

Adding drawings to a watercolour painting is a great idea. But the pressure of perfection scares many new artists. Tracing paper removes the risk of ruining your already amazing artwork. Sketch yourself some smiling fish. Then trace them once they're just the way you want them!

Rubbed off

Watercolour paper has a special layer of gum that helps it absorb paint. If you use a rubber on watercolour paper, you also rub off some of that layer.

To skip the rubbing step, use graphite transfer paper. This paper is already coated with graphite. Just place the image over the graphite paper and trace.

1 Brush paper with wet brush until the paper no longer absorbs water.

2 Use a fan brush to apply a wash of blue paint. Let it dry.

3 Draw fish onto the tracing paper using a graphite pencil.

4 Turn tracing paper over. Using the side of your pencil, rub graphite all over the back of your drawing. Rub the graphite with a tissue or cotton wool ball. Blow or shake off any extra graphite dust.

5 Cut out each fish.

6 Turn the tracing paper back over so the rubbed graphite is on the bottom. Place fish onto the painted paper. Arrange them however you like.

7 Using your pencil, re-trace your fish. This will transfer the fish onto the painted paper. Trace hard enough to transfer your lines without scratching your watercolour paper.

Avoid using blunt pencils when tracing your fish. Sharp pencils will make clear, easy-to-see lines.

Reshaping your brushes

If your brushes look too ragged for this project, try reshaping them.

First, wash your brush in hot, soapy water until the bristles soften. Then gently shape the bristles the way you want. Dip the softened bristles into a gentle shampoo or hair gel. Then allow the brush to air dry.

After the brush is dry, rinse gently until no soap remains.

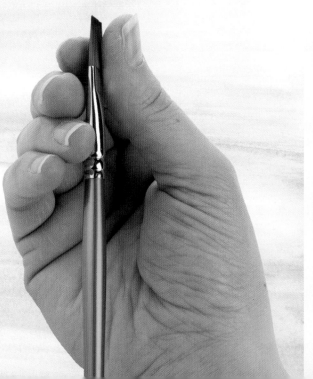

Keep your drawings simple. Too many lines can smudge once you start painting. This can make your watercolours appear muddy.

9

8 Use a round-tip brush to paint the fish. Test out contrasting colours and multiple washes. This will help bring your fish to life.

9 Add details, such as scales and gills, to the fish with a liner brush.

10 Add waves and bubbles to the water.

Cityscape

It's easy to paint your favourite photo with watercolours. But why make an exact copy? Instead, focus on the space's lights and darks (values), shades (tones) and basic shapes.

1. Create the background wash. Use a fan brush and green and blue paints.

2. Add the basic shapes of the trees in the foreground.

3. Add a variety of colour tones to represent the trees in the background. Don't be concerned with shape or size. Just focus on the light and dark areas.

4. Add more layers of colour to the grass and sky.

5. Using a flat brush, add rectangles of colour. These will represent the buildings. Focus on the shapes of the buildings, not the buildings themselves.

6. Continue adding layers of colour. Focus on the shadowed sides of the buildings.

Show-off

Thin mat boards both protect and show off your art. Mat boards have a back piece and a front piece. The front piece has a window cut out of it to frame your artwork.

Watercolours for show are usually matted and framed. Clear sheets of glass or plastic, called glazing, protect your art from dirt and natural light. For extra protection, a varnish made of beeswax can be added.

For best results, hang paintings in a temperature-controlled area. Keep them out of direct sunlight.

7. Use a liner brush to add shape to the background trees.

8. Add leaves and branches to the trees in the foreground.

31

Read more

Landscapes (Brushes with Greatness), Valerie Bodden (Creative Paperbacks, 2013)

Paint It! (Art Smart), Kath Durkin (QED Publishing, 2013)

The Bird King: An Artist's Notebook, Shaun Tan (Arthur A. Levine Books, 2013)

Websites

www.art-is-fun.com/how-to-watercolor.html
This website will be really useful if you need more hints and tips about how to paint with watercolours!

www.teachartathome.com/watercolors.html
If you enjoyed the watercolour projects from this book, how about trying out some more? Visit this website to learn how to paint everything from birds to fish.

www.how-to-draw-and-paint.com/watercolor-paints.html
This website will teach you about the different things you need when painting with watercolours.

Author bio

Mari Bolte is an author of children's books and a lover of art. She lives in southern Minnesota, USA, with her husband, daughter and two dogs. A degree in creative writing has taught her the value of fine writing. Parenthood has made her a purveyor of fine art, with specializations in pavement chalk, washable markers and glitter glue.

Illustrator bio

D.C. Ice has more than a decade of experience as an illustrator of children's books and an artist, with an emphasis on painting. Animals with human attributes are the stars of her illustrations and paintings. As a member of a gallery in St. Paul, Minnesota, USA, and a frequent exhibitor in multiple galleries throughout the country, her love of all things art continues to grow. D.C. received her Bachelor's Degree in Fine Arts from the College of Visual Arts in St. Paul.